WOOD FROG

David M. Schwartz is an award-winning author of children's books, on a wide variety of topics, loved by children around the world. Dwight Kuhn's scientific expertise and artful eye work together with the camera to capture the awesome wonder of the natural world.

Please visit our web site at: www.garethstevens.com
For a free color catalog describing Gareth Stevens Publishing's list of high-quality books
and multimedia programs, call 1-800-542-2595 (USA) or 1-800-461-9120 (Canada).
Gareth Stevens Publishing's Fax: (414) 332-3567.

Library of Congress Cataloging-in-Publication Data

Schwartz, David M.
    Wood frog / by David M. Schwartz; photographs by Dwight Kuhn. — North American ed.
      p. cm. — (Life cycles: a springboards into science series)
    Includes bibliographical references and index.
    ISBN 0-8368-2981-6 (lib. bdg.)
    1. Wood frog—Juvenile literature. [1. Wood frog. 2. Frogs.] I. Kuhn, Dwight, ill.
  II. Title.
  QL668.E27S39   2001
  597.8'92—dc21   2001031465

This North American edition first published in 2001 by
Gareth Stevens Publishing
A Member of the WRC Media Family of Companies
330 West Olive Street, Suite 100
Milwaukee, WI 53212 USA

First published in the United States in 1999 by Creative Teaching Press, Inc., P.O. Box 2723, Huntington Beach, CA 92647-0723.
Text © 1999 by David M. Schwartz; photographs © 1999 by Dwight Kuhn. Additional end matter © 2001 by Gareth Stevens, Inc.

Gareth Stevens editor: Mary Dykstra

Printed in the United States of America

2 3 4 5 6 7 8 9 10 09 08 07 06

WOOD FROG

by David M. Schwartz
photographs by Dwight Kuhn

A SPRINGBOARDS INTO
SCIENCE
SERIES

Gareth Stevens Publishing
A WORLD ALMANAC EDUCATION GROUP COMPANY

It's spring, and you are walking in the woods. Suddenly, a small brown frog hops across your path. Its hind legs are large and strong. The frog has bulging eyes, with a black patch behind each eye. It is a wood frog.

In spring, wood frogs
head for nearby ponds to
find mates. A male wood
frog puffs out its throat
and makes loud croaking
noises. A female hears the
croaks and finds the male.

To mate with the female, the male clasps her from behind. Then the female lays thousands of tiny eggs in a clump of jelly, and the male fertilizes the eggs.

Each egg looks like a tiny dot. Each dot is one cell. After an egg is fertilized, the cell divides into two cells. Then each of those cells divides in two again, making four cells. Those four cells divide into eight cells.

The cells keep dividing. Soon there are many cells in a long, thin shape with a tail at one end and a mouth at the other end. The cells have become a tiny tadpole.

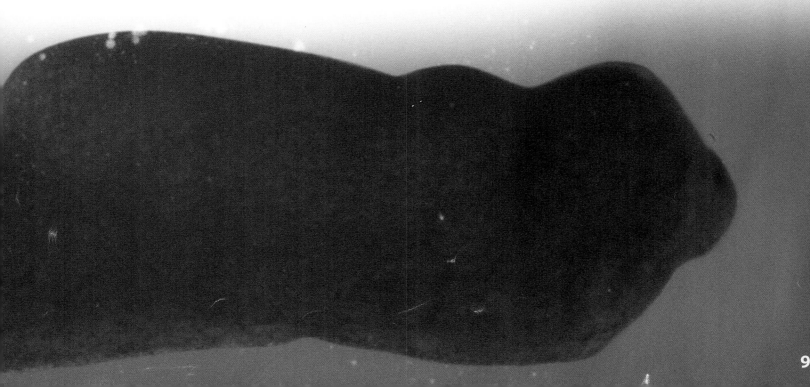

The clump of jelly is full of tiny tadpoles, or pollywogs. After about a week, they wriggle free. The tadpoles look more like fish than frogs!

11

Like a fish, a tadpole swims by waving its tail from side to side. And, like a fish, it breathes underwater through gills.

A tadpole has tiny teeth so it can eat pond plants, such as slimy green algae.

As a tadpole grows, its body changes. First, hind legs appear, then front legs. Then the tadpole's tail begins to shrink.

Inside the tadpole's body, lungs are forming so the tadpole will be able to breathe air. This young frog is almost ready to leave the pond.

When a young frog hops onto dry land, it looks like an adult frog, only smaller. It lives in the woods, eating insects and other small animals. Sometimes it hides under stones or dead leaves so it won't become food for a snake, a raccoon, or any other predator. When danger is near, it quickly hops away.

After a few years, the young frog becomes an adult. One spring day, it will head for a woodland pond to find a mate and start a new generation of wood frogs.

Can you put these steps in
the life cycle of a wood
frog in order?

Answer

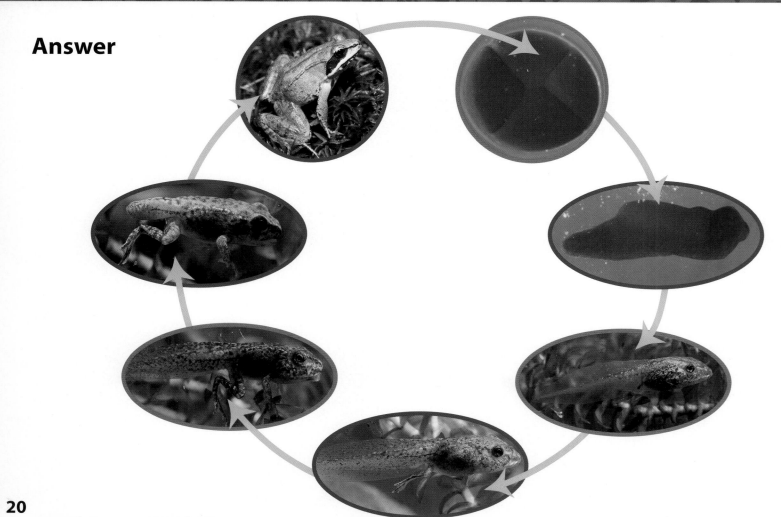

GLOSSARY

algae: tiny water plants without roots, stems, or leaves, which grow in groups that form pond scum and some kinds of seaweed.

bulging: curving or swelling outward.

cell: the smallest and most basic part of an animal or a plant.

clasps: holds an object tightly by reaching or wrapping arms, legs, fingers, or toes around the object.

clump: a thick lump or cluster of solid or almost solid material.

croaking: making a low, hollow sound deep in the throat.

divides: separates into two or more parts.

fertilizes: brings male and female cells together so a new plant or animal can grow.

generation: all of the young that are born during a particular time period.

gills: the organs, or body parts, through which fish and many other water animals breathe.

hind: back or rear.

mates (n): the males or females in pairs of animals that come together to produce young; **(v)** joins together to produce young.

predator: an animal that hunts other animals for food.

wriggle: move quickly in short bursts from side to side; wiggle; squirm.

21

ACTIVITIES

Amazing Amphibians

A wood frog is an amphibian, which is an animal that lives both on land and in the water at different times during its life cycle. Newts and salamanders are amphibians, too, and their life cycles are a lot like a frog's. Use books and web sites to learn more about these amazing amphibians and how they change from eggs to adults. Then draw the steps in the life cycle of a newt or a salamander.

Frog Finding Tour

With an adult, visit a pond, a river, or a lake to look for frogs. A good frog finder has to look very carefully. Sometimes you will see only bulging eyes sticking out of the water. If you don't see any frogs, be very quiet and listen for frog sounds. How would you describe the sounds frogs make? Try comparing them to familiar sounds, such as a rubbing your finger over the edge of a comb or plucking a banjo string. When you get home, write down all the frog sights and sounds you found. If you saw any frogs up close, draw pictures of them and try to find out what kinds of frogs they are.

Make a Pond Viewer

To see what's happening where tadpoles live, make a pond viewer. Have an adult help you cut the bottom and top off of a half-gallon (2-liter) milk carton. Stretch plastic wrap tightly across the bottom of the carton and hold the wrap in place with a tight-fitting rubber band. Take your viewer to a pond. Be sure to take an adult along, too! Carefully lower the wrapped end of the viewer into the water and hold your face up to the open end to look through. Do you see any eggs, tadpoles, or frogs?

More Books to Read

Fabulous Frogs. Linda Glaser (Millbrook Press)
Frogs: Living in Two Worlds. Secrets of the Animal World (series). Andreu Llamas (Gareth Stevens)
From Tadpole to Frog. How Things Grow (series). Jan Kottke (Children's Press)
It's a Frog's Life! Nature Close-Ups (series). Densey Clyne (Gareth Stevens)
A New Frog: My First Look at the Life Cycle of an Amphibian. Pamela Hickman (Kids Can Press)
Tale of a Tadpole. Eyewitness Readers (series). Karen Wallace (DK Publishing)

Videos

All About Amphibians. Animal Life for Children (series). (Schlessinger Media)
The Magic School Bus Hops Home. (Warner)
See How They Grow: Pond Animals. (DK Vision)

Web Sites

jajhs.kana.k12.wv.us/vwv/animal/rep_amph/woodfrog.htm
www.geocities.com/TheTropics/1337/
www.kiddyhouse.com/Themes/frogs/frogs.html

Some web sites stay current longer than others. For additional web sites, use a good search engine to locate the following topics: *amphibians, frogs, ponds, tadpoles,* and *wood frogs.*

INDEX